Dance, You Monster, to My Soft Song

•••

David Starkey

FUTURECYCLE PRESS

www.futurecycle.org

Cover photo, "Torch Lilies" by David Starkey; author photo by Stephen Starkey; cover and interior book design by Diane Kistner; ITC Legacy Sans text with Bodoni Sans titling

Library of Congress Control Number: 2020950586

Published by FutureCycle Press
Athens, Georgia, USA

ISBN 978-1-952593-11-6

What is
My name? Where am I coming from? Where am I going?
A fusillade of question marks.

—Ciaran Carson, "Belfast Confetti"

For Sandy

Contents

Part I

Part II

Part III

Part IV

Epilogue

Part I

Après Nous Le Déluge

These conjunctions leave us wondering:

a young man up to his waste in fetid water
watching placidly as Mamaw sits in her half-
flooded Aerostar, smoking Tareytons,
waiting for help.
                    Maybe it will arrive with the Rapture
or the Revolution, when good people
rally together around a man-
god who foresees their failings and desires
and makes them into words
and bullets and design.
                    This happens
and that happens, and if there's no causality
involved, well tell it to the preacher,
though I don't think he'll be listening this morning
what with the basement of the Free Will
Baptist church submerged
and the whole durned month turning hellish—
never mind the Sunday sun shining
on his whitewashed spire.
                    Then someone pulls
the cord on an outboard motor. There's a whiff
of exhaust as he pilots his johnboat
into the transformed world:
                    left
at Piggly Wiggly, right at Hardee's,

straight on to the still-rising river.

Pilot Light

*...and, behold, the bush burned with fire, and the bush
was not consumed.*
                    —Exodus 3.2

Darkness had always been his comfort,

but he could no longer stomach it
without a couple of 357s. Then he'd loll for hours

on the sagging sofa, ignoring the smell of cat piss

and sour milk while staring at the fire
burning in back of the oven's missing drawer—a little live thing

that sometimes flickered, but hadn't yet gone out.

Mostly, he was too numb for terror,
although recently the long-gone cat had returned,

singing in the flute-like voice of an angel,

and last night, when he was so high on Norco
his ears were screaming, the face of God exploded

from the pilot light, thundering: *This is holy ground!*

His trailer hummed with a honeyed light
that shone beyond the wilderness.

Later, when they pulled his charred corpse

from the wreckage, his cousin reckoned,
He was what he was, remarking on the fact

that the only unburnt items were his shoes.

Necessity

She broods in her dark
rambling house,
and her brood takes
its measure by her tone.
Centuries may pass
until they have sopped up
every last drop
of her bitterness, then
she sends them out
into the unready world,
singly, like sin:
the Pear of Anguish,
the IQ test, books
of divine whisperings,
the cotton gin.

Damascus

Three women are gathered round
a cooking pot in the basement

of a bombed-out apartment block.
In the dim light and woodsmoke

they might be the witches
of *MacBeth,* plotting mischief,

or a trio of fairy godmothers
concocting redemption

for their heroine. They might
even be the silver-haired Fates

weaving our common destiny,
if they weren't simply three

wives who'd lost their husbands
to the incivility of war.

The roads outside are snarled
with converts to violence,

every tomorrow is now past,
but this tenebrous cellar

is almost peaceful as the three
widows wait silently

for a bowl of rice and lentils
before deciding where to go next.

Christic Destroys His Cross

—after Orozco

A man stands on earthquake rubble
    swinging an ax at his fate
as though it were a small cedar tree.
The guards have fled, the crowds
    dispersed like sparrows scattering

from a circling hawk. Beyond
    all reason, he has refused
complicity in his own oblation,
wrenched the rusty nails from his palms
    and nearly completed the unforgivable work.

The sky glowers with patriarchal
    menace, but he's certain of only
two things now: the soul can't ache
with half as much precision as the body,
    and Bibles make good kindling.

More So the Christians

And the reason that was so unfair—everybody was persecuted,
in all fairness—but they were chopping off the heads of everybody,
but more so the Christians. And I thought it was very, very unfair.
—Donald J. Trump, Jan. 17, 2017

So much blood, you walked in there
and it was like walking into a carwash,

but you weren't getting clean, no,

you were getting spattered and splattered
with the hot blood shooting out

of countless necks, although, in all fairness,

some of those necks belonged to mothers
and children worshipping their alien

god, and you did have to feel bad for them,

in a way, but the heads that were *really*
getting chopped off—and, again,

let's be clear, everyone's heads were barreling

down the conveyor belt like in that recent
documentary about a chocolate factory

where the machine spits candies out

so fast these two women (fabulous American
workers, by the way) have to stuff them

in their mouths and down their shirts—

were Christian heads, and, let's face it,
folks, there's just something so tremendous

about even an *average* Christian head

that you really have to place it
in a special category, as opposed

to the many, many other types of heads.

Historical Jesus

A band name.

•

A badge of honor for certain atheists.

•

A highway sign outside Haifa: *Birthplace Just Ahead.*

•

A hitchhiker at a Sonol gas station in the Judean foothills.

•

Parable-bundler.

•

Poet of Aramaic, language of commerce and empire.

•

Eschatologist.

•

A mash-up of sayings from Seneca the Younger and Philo of Alexandria, interpreter of angels.

•

A peddler on the Via Dolorosa.

•

A quest.

•

A cypher.

•

A jumbled alphabet.

•

A gun.

A Curse on Several Priests

When you listened to the choir
Did your old loins burn like hellfire?
Did each young face make you perspire?
Do you still hear them, Father McGuire?
    God send you to your just reward.

What was it made you go berserk?
Their innocence? Their gowns' lacework?
Did you consider them a perk
Of a taxing job, Father Burke?
    God send you to your just reward.

When you gave them their first joyride
Did they tremble as you sighed?
Did you comfort them when they cried?
Did they need you, Father McBride?
    God send you to your just reward.

Do you remember each caress,
Each time you told them to undress?
What was it you wanted to possess?
Did you attain it, Father Hess?
    God send you to your just reward.

Did you feed them cheap champagne,
And whisper words soft and profane,
And wipe away each fresh bloodstain?
Was it delightful, Father Payne?
    God send you to your just reward.

Phoenix

Every morning, a raven drops a crust of bread
at the feet of Saint Paul the Hermit,
who sits all day against a cinderblock wall
on Indian School Road.

Sometimes he eats the bread,
sometimes it is snatched away by a rat
or another man or another raven.

It's the desert,
                but he's not alone—
cars pass by, monotonous as wind,
neighborhood boys kick his bare feet and shins.
Once a week, the police roust him
with a few blows to his ancient skull,

but he's back soon enough,
                       waiting
for God knows what. He stares up
at the horrible blazing sky with the passion
of a man who wants only to forget.

When he dies, who will bury him?
And where? The ground around here
is as hard as a well-lived life.
                    No, harder.

Saint Martin in Dollar General

Here he comes in his Roman soldier outfit,
riding down the Kitchen Wares aisle,
knocking over spatulas and oven mitts
on a horse.
                    Feature that—a horse in Dollar General!
Gladware topples from the shelves, rolls
of aluminum foil spool in front of him
as though it were Christmas,
but it's not Christmas, it's July!

What a mess!

The manager tries to halt his progress,
but he's turned up Home Décor
and now Mr. Ed is breaking mirrors
and knocking assorted plastic lamps to the floor.

Where is the miracle?
                    everyone wants to know.
What is the meaning of this visitation?
but Saint Martin can't be bothered
with wonders or explanations.

He's too busy wrecking Automotive,
this fucking pony of his stomping
on the windshield wiper fluid,
kicking quarts of motor oil.

Saint Sebastian in Starbucks

Saint Sebastian pushes in wearing nothing
but a loincloth, one arrow poking through his torso,
the other out his neck.
     It's all about the greenbacks now,
but this *is* San Francisco: let him do what he wants.

He orders a Grande Dark Roast with room,

nestles into a comfortable low-slung chair,
breathing the fragrance of Rwanda
and Columbia, browsing the *Weekly,*

on which he has spilled a drop or two of blood.

Is there a sense the world's slightly less chaotic?
A moment when everyone's phones flicker dead?

A few sidelong glances from the other customers—
he may be a martyr,
but he's washboard-ripped with golden locks:

he still looks *good.*

Outside, the rumbling of the Market Street buses,
workers flocking

into a grand building adorned with a little blue bird.

Meanwhile, the orders keep on coming:
Short Caffè Americano,
Skinny Venti Vanilla Latte,
Tall Iced Flat White,

hold the ice.

Dance, You Monster, to My Soft Song

—After Klee

Candles burn in a menorah
atop a rickety spinet.
                              Music
clanks and rolls from the keys,
quiet yet cacophonous—

just the sort of tune to make a monster rise
from the earth and waggle
its tiny feet.
                    Sway and twirl,
you comic beast of dreams!
                                    You
with your bright pink penis nose,
your wide and unbelievable eyes!

Part II

I Am North Highlands

I won't go back to it....
            —Evan Boland, "Mise Éire"

I'll stay away from the cars parked on the street
                and on the desiccated lawns
        from the pale blue '68 bug
                        rusting in someone's driveway
next to a speedboat and a disused washing machine

        From mulberry and olive trees and the white-
flowered oleander and the tire swing hanging
        from a willow oak
                    and sour gums shriveling for lack of water

I won't go home to the plastic lawn chairs
                        tipped over on the back porch
        the back fences falling down
                    the doughboy pool filled with rotting leaves

                The doll with a missing head
        the tricycle with only two wheels
the punctured basketball

                I prefer a full night's sleep
to three Harleys idling at the corner at 2 a.m.
                    a semi rumbling to life at 4

        No I'll stay away
precisely because the place is as much a part of me
                as the Doberman-
Shepherd mix barking incessantly in the side yard
the American flags fluttering above the weeds
                the Christmas lights that hang all year
                        from unpainted eaves

because the words I can't keep from my mouth
clot my tongue whenever I want to wax eloquent
about virtue and vice
      justice and theology
           necessity

and contingency

whenever in short I want to rinse the ash
   and offal from my tongue
      and talk about anything but the same old shit

Homemade Ice Cream

My grandmother peels, pits and chops
the bag of peaches, fresh from the Kroger
on Laurel Avenue, pureeing them
in her Waring blender, as my grandfather fills
the sides of the hand-cranked ice cream maker
with crushed ice and rock salt.

Beaumont, Texas, 1968. The world
is exploding, but my grandparents are doing their best
to seal the change inside the black and white TV
in their living room. Still, I can hear the music
coming from the big, ramshackle house
behind theirs—loud and angry, and not white at all.

They fill the stainless steel cannister with peaches,
condensed milk, sugar and vanilla, and the long
process begins. Everyone takes a turn—
Mom, Dad, even my little sister,
who can barely grasp the handle.

It seems to take forever.

They are so poor, I will learn later,
and so angry at their poverty.
They say things about their neighbors,
horrible things I do not want to repeat.
And yet on this July night well past the pivot
point of the American century, we are all laughing,
clapping our hands when the mixture finally thickens
enough to eat. It is so good, I can almost taste it
fifty years later—so creamy, so rich, so sweet.

Ugly Word

I was eight. I knew it was an ugly word,
        low and mean, but I was flush with fascination
     for the argot I heard from the older kids
on my street, hucksterish teens with freaky hair
and clothes, who frittered away the evenings
     smoking cigarettes, rocking back and forth

on their flat feet, explaining the havoc
        of the world with a flourish of their hands
     and a fillip of fortune-teller style.
The ladies in the bridge club were momentarily
speechless—a kind of miracle in itself—
     then one laughed, another clucked sadly.

My dumbstruck mother frowned, sent me to my room
        with a silent scolding. In our neighborhood,
     what could you expect? I fretted over
my fatheadedness for a while, then let it go,
and when they'd all left and she was asleep,
     I snuck out the window and lammed it back

to the corner sideshow, eager to reenter
        that linguistic limbo, that alphabet soup
     of lingo both patriarchal and infantile.
How I loved their pluck and flimflam,
the fevered tongue of those still deciding
     whether it was luckier to be saved or damned....

Delivering Phone Books

Pale and heavily pregnant,
my probable wife-to-be
drove the Datsun pick-up
slowly up and down the blocks.

I'd slice open the shrink wrap
with an X-Acto knife
and trot back and forth
from truck bed to porch,

one thick directory
in each hand, one beneath
each arm. 1985
and everyone I knew

was poised to make a mint,
while I, who had spent
my entire life not planning,
prepared to succumb

to my great mistake. Nights,
I'd wake, dry-throated
and shivering, but escape
seemed ignoble. Therefore,

I took the job,
though it was temporary
and paid piece rate.
She had my number,

watching in the rearview mirror
as I went about my work,
her pale green eyes glistening
and vengeful.

Posturepedic

A bad omen, that mattress
　　we bought at the Salvation Army
　　　　and took back to our rented

rat-trap, strapped to the top
　　of my Mercury Monterey. Yes,
　　　　it was only twenty bucks, but the coils

poked through the fabric, which reeked
　　of mildew, and it was too big
　　　　for the box spring so it kept slipping

to the cold wood floor. We'd wake
　　night after night spilled atop
　　　　one another like two acrobats

fallen from their wire. Outside,
　　winter rain clanged against
　　　　the aluminum awnings. Mornings

I'd wake to find her staring at me
　　like a jailor who wasn't sure
　　　　she'd locked the door. I began

plotting my escape, although
　　it would take years to execute, although
　　　　we'd only been married ten days.

A Brief History of My First Marriage

1988

The year George Herbert Bush was chosen
to take Ronald Reagan's place,
she and I finally united our two incompatible
states with vows of wedlock.
A broken clock

didn't tick on the walls of the Sacramento
County Courthouse. Beneath it,
a large framed photograph of two gophers
in nuptial attire.
It felt like we were applying for a building permit.

Nothing about that afternoon seemed right—
just a slow, creeping sense Hel
was inching closer.
We spent our lone honeymoon night
at the Red Lion Inn.

1991

In South Carolina, we rented a brick house
across from the Greenwood
Baptist Church. A yard for the kids
and the mutt she'd rescued from the fire station
where the firemen were stoning it. Moss

covered the roof I'd sometimes ascend
to drink a beer while she yelled in the rooms below.
If I was lucky, the squeaking of the rusty
attic vent would deaden her voice.
A few blocks away, the glow

and rumble of traffic on Claussen Road.
Pine needles fell like her tears,
routinely and thick enough to blanket
the ground. Every morning I had to recommit
to a future in which I was there.

1993

Finally, a diagnosis: Rapid
Cycling Bipolar Disorder with Ultradian
Rhythms. Our muddled, angry
life had a name.
And so our unhappy

family scraped by—
just. The checkbook never balanced.
We used the gas card for bread
and milk. The pre-recorded church bells chimed.
Our '72 Mercury blew a head

gasket and expired. Meanwhile, the doctor tinkered,
unsuccessfully, with her meds.
One day, she'd be almost fine.
The next, she'd be crying uncontrollably,
flinging plates against the wall.

1994

She tried to kill herself by gulping a fistful of Ativan
and Effexor while *A Trip*
to Bountiful played on the VCR.
Frantic, I half-
carried her to the car

and drove her to the hospital.
While they pumped her stomach, I
read a 1976 edition of *Reader's Digest:* "Arthur Mitchell's
Dance to Glory"
and "Why Jimmy Hoffa Had to Die."

When they let me in to see her, a plastic tube
full of black bile
was poking from one nostril.
Her face was red as raw steak.
The nurse told her, "It's okay, Hon. We all make mistakes."

1998

Suddenly, I began weeping.
Back porch of my parents' home: August,
a few days before returning
to Illinois. A dog barked. The sprinklers
in the neighbor's yard came on. The grief seeping

for years had finally burst.
I told them I couldn't be married anymore.
They weren't surprised.
Immediately, we began plotting my getaway.
The kids came outside, sensing something astray.

But I couldn't go through with it. Guilt and practicalities:
the only affordable place I could find
in the Western Suburbs was a studio apartment
overlooking a tollway embankment.
Wherefore we remained entangled, like coiling kudzu vines.

2000

In April, at a conference, I met someone else.
Not love,
but *true* love.
Without hesitation,
I told her I was moving out.

I threw my forty cents into the final basket
on the East-West Tollway and drove
like hell for California. She wanted me in a casket,
buried with my new trove
of happiness.

The war was on.
Her paramount objective was to drag me
down
into her sea of hatred.
My only goal was not to drown.

Decapitations

Shortly after our divorce,
my ex went through hundreds
of family photographs
and snipped off all my heads.

There I am at Christmas,
headless, and headless, too,
at our daughters' birthdays
and the backyard barbecue.

Headless at Easter, bending
down to grasp a purple egg,
and headless in new-fallen snow
(she's also cut off my leg).

She sent three bulky envelopes
through the U.S. mail,
along with a twenty-page
letter that went into great detail

about my many failings
as a husband and a dad.
You're lucky to be alive, she said,
and, indeed, I'm very glad.

Every Thing Good Is on the Highway

—Emerson

Willie Nelson and tumbleweeds,
     No Passing signs and copses
of willow trees, barns in twilight
and soybean fields, pumpkins
     for sale—a dollar apiece—bales

of still green hay, barbed wire
     and mobile homes, saguaro cactus
and fireworks stores, dust storms
and flash floods, moose crossings
     and railroad crossings and empty

crossroads and traffic lights,
     a hundred thousand thousand
gas stations, derelict souvenir
stands and clouds of deer
     flies and twenty-five miles

of barrenness, telephone poles
     and grain silos and the insomniac
bliss of late August at midnight—
the acid swirl of Northern lights
     when the equinoctial spirit

dance teases toward asphalt,
     the solar wind never quite
touching us with its lovely
otherworldly hues: green
     and pink and red and, lastly, blue.

In the Hall of Bronzes
at the Pro Football Hall of Fame

It's dark but for the spotlights
reflecting off each stoical
or smiling face absorbed
by some past autumnal
miracle. We acolytes whisper

in the presence of so much majesty,
yet stripped of helmets
and team insignia,
they have become human men,
as mortal as those of us

who try to their catch steely gazes
or return their swaggering grins.
They all seem proud to be here
among this silent company—
forgotten running backs

from the Rock Island Independents
and the Oorang Indians, guards
and tackles who were rewarded
for their dementia with little
more than the admiration of their peers.

Accompanied by my son
and the spirit of my father,
I pass the heroes of my youth
frozen in one final valiant
pose: George Blarda, ageless

and ancient, ruthless
Willie Brown, gentlemanly
Bob Lily, sad-eyed

Fran Tarkenton, defeated
　　　　　in every championship game,

　　　and O.J. Simpson, whose broken-
　　　　　　　field run to prison doesn't keep him
　　　from meeting each new pair
of disapproving eyes—year
　　　　　after tarnished year—straight on.

Birds

Sick on a visit to my parents' house, I lie
      in bed listening through the open window
    to the sounds of the old neighborhood:
a hose washing down a driveway, a lawnmower
    guttering out, two guys arguing about how to fix
      the engine of their car, which dies after exactly—
one, two, three, four, five, six—seven
    seconds every time they start it up.

If I stood on the roof of my old house
      I could throw a tennis ball and hit the homes
    of two child molesters: the one across the street
now in prison—most likely until he's dead—the other
    escaped, despite his star turn on *America's*
    Most Wanted. As a boy, I thought the two
of them—steady civilian workers at the military
    base—no different than any other men.

Don't mistake me: I wasn't one of those
      touched, but my sister was, and she carries
    that memory with her. Sometimes it's as portable
as a paper sack of rocks, but other times it's as pervasive
    as the dark matter between stars. Those days,
      she locks herself up in her room. My father
says he'll shoot the son-of-a-bitch himself
    if he ever makes it past the parole board.

Honestly, though, I don't spend much time
      thinking of my hometown or my childhood—
    obliviousness a marvelous luxury.
For months at a time, I simply stay away.
    And though I'm ill now, in a day or two,
      my fever will break, the dull aching

in my bones will subside, and I will leave
       this small room and the traffic noise

    from the freeway two blocks away, which pounds
        through the screen like heavy rain. As I get up
      to close the window, there's a curse and a slamming
car door—the two guys give up on their jalopy.
    And then, strangely, I hear birdsong.
      I had forgotten there were birds here,
though of course in a place with trees
      and water, birds would be there, too.

Part III

Occupations

Able Seaman

It's crowded this evening, the other ships in the harbor tooting their horns as you make for open water. You've already chipped the rust from the superstructure, stowed the stationary rigging, sounded the rare unfamiliar depths, scrubbed the wheelhouse and the quarterdeck. All that's left is to escape this bottleneck of frigates and trawlers, tankers and hydrofoils. You stand on the bow with your red and yellow semaphore flags: left hand down, right hand low; left hand out, right hand high across. You can't, for the life of you, remember what any of it means, and the other ships are getting closer.

Door Assembler

On the warehouse floor, the necessary components of your trade are arrayed around you like pieces of a mosaic: lock blocks and handles, hinges, nails and screws. You hear your favorite aria coming from the parking lot: "Un bel di vedremo" from *Madama Butterfly*. The windows are open to the warm spring air. Birdsong and the scent of wisteria and plumeria and wild thyme. You pick up your rivet gun. You point it at your head.

Honey Processor

You seed the honey with crystals, then stir the mixture in a vat big enough to house a hundred thousand bees. You adjust the pasteurizing temperature. You fiddle with the blending valves. You sample the merchandise with the tip of your little finger, squint a bit—too sweet. You quietly ascend and descend a dozen ladders. The warehouse where you work is strangely silent, like a meadow without clover, a desert without wind.

Icicle Machine Operator

You stand at your machine all day, dreaming of Ecuador, dreaming of the Virgin Islands and the Hanging Gardens of Babylon. Meanwhile, tubes of cellophane approach you on the conveyor belt. You fill them with the artificial flavors of strawberries and bananas and oranges. You adjust the spindle counterweights. You fuse the seams of cellophane. The foreman slowly paces behind you and the others, like the judge at Westminster Kennel Club charged with deciding best in show. The factory smells of machine grease and sawdust and blueberries. You turn to stretch your neck and sweet water spills on the concrete. The foreman stares at you. Your co-workers stare. The conveyor belt continues moving at its indifferent, processional pace.

Joy Loader

The machine you operate is enormous, loud and orange. The rumble of crushers and conveyors, the tumbling of coal. Your lights play against the mine shaft, slashing at the reluctant darkness. Your face—where it's not covered by helmet, goggles and mask—is bathed in inky dust. You work the levers, operate the winch, pry loose a glossy chunk of anthracite from the gathering-arm teeth. Someone calls you from the surface on the two-way radio, but you don't recognize the voice.

Ornament Maker

All summer long, Christmas: painting snowflakes on glass balls, tying ribbons atop plastic bells, gluing eyes on reindeer, bending artificial boughs into wreaths the size of monster truck tires. Outside, the neighbor kids are playing in the sprinklers, while their English bulldog, Blue, is shitting on your sun-killed lawn. You twist the arms of an elf with needle-nose pliers, play *Elvis' Christmas Album:* "Here Comes Santa Claus," "It Is No Secret (What God Can Do)."

Oyster Shucker

The short and heavy-handled knife feels good in your gloved grip as you shove the shell inside the shucking block and sever the muscles holding the halves together. You slide the blade beneath the meat, then let it rest on one pearly side in a bed of ice. The other half goes in the trash. Through the slatted window above the metal sink where you work, you can see the tourists wandering the harbor. An old man rests against the railing, staring at the swaying boats. One couple kisses in the shadow of your restaurant; another couple's arguing.

Unattended Ground Sensor Specialist

Your superior plays *Monument Valley* on his phone as you emplace the surveillance devices. While you compute density, direction and rate of movement, he plays *Ridiculous Fishing* and *Device 6*. The nature of the conflict is evolving by the moment, the urgency of the situation cannot be exaggerated. You want to say to him, *Sir, I recommend supporting fire on the targets. Sir, the coordinates have changed.* But he is your superior and he is otherwise engaged.

Venetian Blind Installer

You might see anything through those slats you're hanging: a madman mouthing silent aphorisms, a child crying on her trike. But it's tranquil now, only a mockingbird motionless in a pepper tree as you drill bracket holes in the casement, test the movement of the slats, try the drawstring, imagine a world without you in it—windowless and deaf and dumb.

Yarn Winder

The yarn factory is a blur and flash of vivid hues: amethyst and cherry red, tangerine and parakeet, grenadine and emerald. You stand at your spindle, threading ends, trimming and packaging your bundles. Every morning, you vow to take up knitting, and every evening you renounce that vow. You'll never merit all this color. All around you are the specialists: the cone spooler and the redraw operator, the cake and bobbin and worsted winders—each of them more skilled and vastly more experienced than you, who have only been winding yarn for twenty years.

Zipper Trimmer

No one stays awake at night dreaming of this job—measuring chains and snipping excess scoops until each strip is perfectly matched to its function, color and design. Pinching out weak links, hooking in the sliders, is the most mindless sort of work, yet who could deny the invention's marvel? Like fire and the wheel, its simplicity belies its endless uses. And there's something deeply satisfying about the way it can reveal forbidden parts, or hide them instantly. *Good night,* it allows anyone to say, *no thanks*— the door shutting, the sound of every tooth locking into place.

Part IV

Mendel: Portrait, with Peas

The long narrow garden: one side shaded
by the white-washed abbey, the other facing

morning sun. Vines tall with white flowers; short
with violet. The yellow seeds, the green.

Delicate glasses perched on a pudgy face.
The pods green or yellow, smooth

or crumpled. Latent and recessive;
dominant and loud. Father

of orange bread mold and the sea squirt,
E. coli and the white-eyed fruit fly.

An oversized cross looped around his neck,
resting on his cassock like a child's house key.

The hairline receding, the expression
wry, never quite blossoming into a smile.

The Death of LBJ

For years his heart had been waiting to capitulate
and now that reliable deceiver
had its chance.
                Lady Bird told him he was beginning
to look just like a hippie, what with his hair curling
down the back of his neck—a barber
was on order. She told him if he waited patiently
while she went into town, she'd make him
a German chocolate cake.
                Pajama-clad, he lay in bed,
fussing with his covers. Somewhere, a chain saw
fired up, then guttered out. The window was open
an inch or two, and an oak tree tapped a branch
against the glass. He leaned over to see it,
leaned closer to hear the murmur
of the Pedernales River.
                O you who believe
help always arrives on command,
know that he died with the telephone receiver
still in his hand.

MMI

Never such innocence again.
　　　　　—Philip Larkin, 'MCMXIV"

People early for work, practically lolling,
　　　　an Americano with a shot in hand. Others
　　　running late, swarming up the stairs
　and escalators from the PATH station,
all of them headed for the banks of elevators,
　　　their day plotted out from end to end.

　Many of us would freeze them there
　　　　if we could, forbid the fretful morning
　　　from ever reaching quarter to nine. Better
　to stash them in a wax museum—like Picasso
and Hemingway at Madame Tussaud's,
　　　huddled together, brooding but undestroyed.

　Some of us, though, would insist that time
　　　　continue ticking, that the foreordained
　　　event collapse in on itself in ash and smoke
　and reams of fluttering office paper, as it has
so often in memory. These fatalists
　　　will accept nothing less than history.

　Yet even the culprits themselves surely
　　　　would not begrudge that final kiss between
　　　husband and wife on Church Street, before
　she hops back into the cab going uptown,
while he tucks his briefcase under his arm
　　　like a football and waits for a car to the 101st floor.

On the Fifteenth Anniversary
of the Death of Derrida

The day begins in fog, mist clinging
to hilltops, birds erratic

in their song. Above the ocean,
air and its attendant wrongs.

Along the coasts of the world,
books have been left out overnight

on wooden tables and in the seats
of plastic chairs, their pages curling

at the corners, letters etched with salt.
On a dew-wet beach in Indonesia,

Rilke's eszetts have lost their sibilance,
and Trakl's umlauts—damp, smeared,

illegible—no longer have the power
to round the vowels they rest upon.

Resilience

—Elizabeth Edwards, 1949-2010

The end near, how unaccountably
tender we felt toward you
and that ill-

fitting wig, your steadfast smile,
the diamond cross
around your neck that seemed more

talisman than crucifix.
Your cancer and philandering
husband had become our problems

as well as yours, though we all knew
they would vanish soon
and as suddenly as snow in heavy rain.

This morning you were "refusing
further treatment"
and by afternoon you were dead—

though a friend says she still expects you
to greet her at your door
with a Diet Coke in one hand,

a cup of yogurt in the other,
a snide quip on your lips,
beckoning: *Come in! Come in!*

Actively Passing

—I. M. Andre Levi, 1959-2012

I took the kayak out this morning
though fog was rolling in,

the wind was picking up

and a dissipating
tropical storm made it difficult to launch

into the break.

Still, I wanted to be away from shore
for an hour

to think about yesterday.

The hospice nurse warned me
before I went into your room:

Be prepared. Some people

find it disturbing. But nighttime crickets
were playing on your iPod,

the room was comfortably dark,

and friends had set up a sort of altar
on the table by your bed:

two candles, books of poetry,

the sequined butterflies
you gave as gifts

to people you felt sorry for.

Your pale face was all but hidden
by a blanket, your breathing

labored and erratic.

I'm sorry that I didn't stay for long.
I felt too keenly the nurse's words,

so apt for all of us—

actively passing from our own lives
when we should be rocking,

rocking on the ocean waves.

The Sinking of the MV *Sewol*

In the swift and changing
currents of the Maenggol
Channel, a sharp turn

to starboard—the ship
listing to port—then hard
back to port. Soon,

the loading bay was flooded,
and the four hundred tons
of iron in the hold—destined

for the naval base—made
righting the *Sewol* impossible.
Ah, well, I heard an old man say,

as we watched the news
at LAX while waiting
for our plane, *they are only lives*

lost. We'll all lose ours someday.
I turned to stare at him,
astonished, and he smiled,

his face heavy with sin,
his eyes like two portholes,
the water rushing in.

The Death of a Confederate Soldier

—for Heather Heyer

Protestors on the ground barely clear the way
before the soldier leaves his granite perch with surprising ease
and takes a header on the courthouse lawn.

His skull collapses into his neck,
legs twist behind his body
like a child landing a bad belly flop.

For a moment, one can almost imagine music:
a Handel violin sonata, say,
swirling thirty-second notes,
    the harpsichord's quiet accompaniment—

then everyone's flipping the soldier the bird,
kicking the fallen thing with their sandals
and running shoes.

Phones are out amid the chants and cheers,
        and why not?

A living, breathing person died,
    but it wasn't here.

Not here, not here.

O, please God, not her.

Elegy, with Lard Biscuits

—JW, 1953-2017

Your mouth would pucker whenever you read
a bad poem, as though you'd swallowed a forkful

of pickled beets. Words were food, and you sniffed

before you tasted, like a man bent over
the pork tenderloin on his barbecue.

You grew up as close to Tennessee as North

Carolina allows, and you loved everything
about those mountains—the fiddlers and trout fishing

and second-cousins who made you laugh

at yourself. But when they began sneering
at your lisp and love of Tennyson, whose poems

you stole from the public library (your only crime),

you decamped for Southern California.
You never went home to that holler

off Hiwassee Lake, but you never left it

either, especially the *cucina povera*
your mother cooked on her woodstove:

turnip greens, collards, sweet potato pie.

Was it only six months ago we sat around
your living room taking turns reading *Chickamauga*

aloud? Dinner was smoked venison—where

on God's green earth had you got hold of *that?*—
buttermilk cabbage soup, summer succotash,

and for dessert, a big bowl of huckleberries

and cream, sprinkled with sugar. You savored
each time-steeped line, just as you rolled the berries

across your tongue, smiling, comically smacking

your lips. Bill Monroe on the stereo.
Surely, your mother would have been pleased.

The Walking Man

—I. M. Tom Post, 1942-2018

In my neighborhood, he was known
as the Walking Man—an early riser, gliding
up the steepest streets as though gravity
had never been invented. On our way to work,
we'd see him as the sun crept over the roofs
of our ranch houses, ascending
Camino Manadero, or cutting across
Camino Cerralvo, his hand raised
in a friendly hello to every passing car.

You might have thought he was too pleasant
to be an artist, but you'd learn
how wrong you were the moment
you looked upon his paintings,
ambiguous, yet certain
about the qualities of color
and how things half-formed and changing
constitute our greatest hope.
You'd see it in canvas after canvas:
the way the world works its magic on us,
like a lazy scrawl of cirrus across the horizon—
dawn morphing into brighter day.

Christmas Eve, 2018

Poinsettias in the windows, Christmas lights strung
across the pepper trees. On some streets, no one

but a local would know a year ago the steep
mountainsides were swathed in flames, the smoke

so thick it wound down into your lungs
like an unspooled skein of cotton. Homes emptied:

you were staying at someone's house, or someone—
and their dogs—had moved in with you. Downtown,

leaves skittered up State Street, as window shoppers
wearing dust masks trod warily in the burnt umber air.

Then, far worse, that early January morning
when rain dowsed the fire but upended the earth,

which raged and churned and roared like the great Flood
come at last to sweep us from the safety of our dreams.

Afterwards, an eerie, birdless quiet and mud,
mud everywhere—on our clothes and in our living rooms,

plastered to the boulders that were suddenly scattered
across the landscape like stars in the night sky.

And where were the people we loved and knew
and who wouldn't answer their phones though we called

and called until our own phones were dead? Some refused
our summons altogether, though days passed, then weeks,

our grief become as constant as the whir and grind
and beeping of heavy machinery, which gradually gave way

to the scraping of shovels as the bucket brigades
began reducing the tragedy to human-scale, one

wheelbarrow at a time. We learned so much
of what we cherish is rubbish that can be bulldozed

into piles and hauled away. It's the lives of others
we cannot live without—though we try, and are trying now.

Tonight, at the Biltmore, two valets laugh companionably
as they wait for their next guests. From the radio

of a car parked alongside Butterfly Beach comes
the redemptive voice of Bing Crosby singing,

"Fall on your knees," while the surf soughs and the wind,
redolent of salt and eucalyptus, whispers of grace.

Epilogue

In the Lion's Cage

Chased by an angry horse, circus hand Charlie Chaplin takes
   refuge, accidentally, in a lion's cage.

An angry mob descends on the Marion City Jail.

The door shuts behind him.

*Armed with sledgehammers, they overwhelm the single deputy, who
   disappears into the night.*

Fortunately, the lion is asleep.

*The mob wants Thomas Shipp and Abram Smith, two black men accused
   of killing a white man and raping his girlfriend.*

Attempting to open the door, Charlie stumbles and locks it.

The mob, naturally, is white.

A trap door in the back of the cage leads to another cage, housing
   a Bengal tiger.

Someone finds the key, inserts it in the lock.

He decides the lion's cage is preferable.

*The two men prepare to defend themselves, but the mob surges forward,
   many-handed and enraged.*

Charlie knocks a tin pan of water from the shelf.

Shipp and Smith are beaten as they are dragged from their cell.

But he catches it before it hits the ground.

Beaten as they are dragged up the steps.

The lion sleeps uneasily.

Beaten as they are dragged onto the Main Street of Marion, Indiana, USA.

A small dog arrives outside the cage, yapping wildly.

A Charlie Chaplin picture is playing at the Bijou.

Charlie begs it to stop: it does not.

But the theater has emptied out: everyone's joined the mob.

He slides his foot between the bars, hoping to give the dog a kick.

By now, the men's clothes are torn and bloody.

Instead, the dog chomps down on Charlie's trouser leg.

Their eyes are swollen shut.

A woman arrives: he begs her to open the door.

Most of the men in the mob are wearing straw hats and workers' caps.

She sees the lion and faints.

The women are dressed for an evening out.

The dog lets go of Charlie's pants and scampers away.

Someone calls for heavy rope.

He splashes water from the pan onto the woman, hoping to revive her.

The owner of the hardware store tells everyone he'll be right back.

It does not work.

There is a pause, a catching of breaths.

The lion yawns and wakes.

Shipp and Smith lie unconscious on the grass.

Charlie flees to a far corner of the cage.

A few bystanders, conscience-stricken, begin to edge away.

The lion follows, sniffs Charlie's crotch, then returns to its spot, stretches out and falls asleep again.

Flasks of whiskey are passed around from man to man, surreptitiously, so as not to upset the ladies.

Charlie breathes a sigh of relief.

The town photographer rushes to his studio.

He is becoming accustomed to his plight.

The owner of the hardware store returns with two coils of thick rope.

The woman finally stirs.

The two necks are carefully measured.

She runs to the cage door and opens it.

No need to tie their hands behind their backs: they're too far gone to put up a fight.

Charlie is blasé: Me? Want to *leave?* Whatever might give you that idea?

The ropes are slung over the arms of two tall elms.

Before he goes, he decides to taunt the lion.

The business is concluded quickly: nooses tightened, bodies raised.

The lion roars and Charlie races from the cage, the woman locking the door behind him.

Shipp and Smith dangle from the trees.

Where has he gone?

The photographer returns, sets up his tripod, ignites his flash powder.

Look: he's climbed the pole holding up the big top.

The lens opens and shuts.

The woman puts her hands on her hips: come down from there, you tramp.

The piano player and the film operator have also left the Bijou to see what's going on.

Not yet: first, Charlie extends his arms, then folds them behind his head, mimicking a high-wire acrobat.

Although no one's there to watch, the film continues playing.

Then he flaps his arms, like a swan, and slides down the pole.

Silently.

Safe at last.

Acknowledgments

Grateful acknowledgement is made to the editors of the following journals in which these poems, sometimes with different titles, first appeared.

American Literary Review: "Ugly Word"
Carbon Culture: "Able Seaman," "Yarn Winder"
Chariton Review: "Phoenix"
Crannóg: "I Am North Highlands"
Descant: "In the Hall of Bronzes at the Pro Football Hall of Fame"
Fourteen Hills: "Unattended Ground Censor Specialist"
Georgia Review: "In the Lion's Cage"
Jelly Bucket: "Posturepedic," "Actively Passing"
Lake Effect: "The Death of LBJ"
Mid-American Review: "MMI"
Miramar: "Historical Jesus"
Pembroke Magazine: "The Death of a Confederate Soldier," "Elegy, with Lard Biscuits"
Prairie Schooner: "Pilot Light"
RE:AL: "Damascus"
Reed Magazine: "The Sinking of the MV *Sewol*"
River Styx: "Birds"
Sakura: "Door Assembler," "Icicle Machine Operator"
Santa Barbara News-Press: "Christmas Eve, 2018"
Santa Barbara View: "Resilience"
Southern California Review: "Christ Destroys His Cross"
Southern Poetry Review: "Mendel: Portrait, with Peas"
Southern Review: "Après Nous Le Déluge," "Homemade Ice Cream"
Tampa Review: "On the Fifteenth Anniversary of the Death of Derrida"
Texas Review: "More So the Christians"
Timberline Review: "Saint Sebastian in Starbucks"
Upstairs at Duroc: "Honey Processor," "Joy Loader," "Oyster Shucker," "Venetian Blind Installer"
Washington Square: "Every Thing Good Is on the Highway"

About FutureCycle Press

FutureCycle Press is dedicated to publishing lasting English-language poetry in both print-on-demand and Kindle formats. Founded in 2007 by long-time independent editor/publishers and partners Diane Kistner and Robert S. King, the press incorporated as a nonprofit in 2012. A number of our editors are distinguished poets and writers in their own right, and we have been actively involved in the small press movement going back to the early seventies.

We award the FutureCycle Poetry Book Prize and honorarium annually for the best full-length volume of poetry we published that year. Introduced in 2013, proceeds from our Good Works projects are donated to charity. Our Selected Poems series highlights contemporary poets with a substantial body of work to their credit; with this series we strive to resurrect work that has had limited distribution and is now out of print.

We are dedicated to giving all of the authors we publish the care their work deserves, offering a catalog of the most diverse and distinguished work possible, and paying forward any earnings to fund more great books. All of our books are kept "alive" and available unless and until an author requests a title be taken out of print.

We've learned a few things about independent publishing over the years. We've also evolved a unique and resilient publishing model that allows us to focus mainly on vetting and preserving for posterity poetry collections of exceptional quality without becoming overwhelmed with bookkeeping and mailing, fundraising activities, or taxing editorial or production "bubbles." To find out more, come see us at www.futurecycle.org.

The FutureCycle Poetry Book Prize

All full-length poetry books published by FutureCycle Press in a calendar year are considered for the annual FutureCycle Poetry Book Prize. This allows us to consider each submission on its own merits, outside of the context of a traditional contest. Too, the judges see the finished book, which will have benefitted from the beautiful book design and strong editorial gloss we are famous for.

The book ranked the best in judging is announced as the prize-winner in the subsequent year. There is no fixed monetary award; instead, the winning poet receives an honorarium of 20% of the total net royalties from all poetry books and chapbooks the press sold online in the year the winning book was published. The winner is also accorded the honor of being on the panel of judges for the next year's competition; all judges receive copies of all contending books to keep for their personal library.

www.ingramcontent.com/pod-product-compliance
Lightning Source LLC
Chambersburg PA
CBHW070010100426
42741CB00012B/3190